6⁹⁸

D1208862

OVER CAPE COD

AND THE ISLANDS

OVER CAPE COD

AND THE ISLANDS

STEPHEN PROEHL

INTRODUCTION BY NORTON H. NICKERSON

HOUGHTON MIFFLIN COMPANY BOSTON 1979

The plate facing the title page is a view
over Pleasant Bay, looking down the arm of the Cape.

Copyright © 1979 by Stephen Proehl

All rights reserved. No part of this work may be reproduced or transmitted
in any form by any means, electronic or mechanical, including photocopying
and recording, or by any information storage or retrieval system, without per-
mission in writing from the publisher.

Library of Congress Cataloging in Publication Data
Proehl, Stephen.
Over Cape Cod and the islands.
Bibliography: p.
1. Cape Cod—Description and travel—Views.
2. Elizabeth Islands, Mass.—Description and travel—
Views. 3. Nantucket, Mass.—Description and travel—
Views. 4. Martha's Vineyard, Mass.—Description and
travel—Views. I. Title.
F72.C3P76   917.44'92   78–26135
ISBN 0–395–27064–2   ISBN 0–395–27937–2 pbk.

Printed in the United States of America

H 10 9 8 7 6 5 4 3 2 1

TO SUSAN

ACKNOWLEDGMENTS

You're only as good as the people you associate with. My wife, Susan, encouraged and supported me throughout the project; her turn is next. Claude and Mildred Hope and Paul and Virginia Proehl stood by patiently. Dean MacIsaac flew the helicopter and put me into places I never dreamed I could go. My editor, Daphne Abeel, showed me new ways of looking at my own work. Dr. Norton Nickerson contributed his vast store of knowledge about the environment of Cape Cod and the Islands. My good friends Dan Dimancescu, Arnie Holtberg, and Ken and Sandra Janes listened to me and gave me perspective. Thanks also to Will and Joyce Garrick, Patricia Parker, Ruth Wise, Grant Ujifusa, Northeast Color Research, and to the entire design and production staff at Houghton Mifflin.

— STEPHEN PROEHL

CONTENTS

ORDER OF THE PLATES

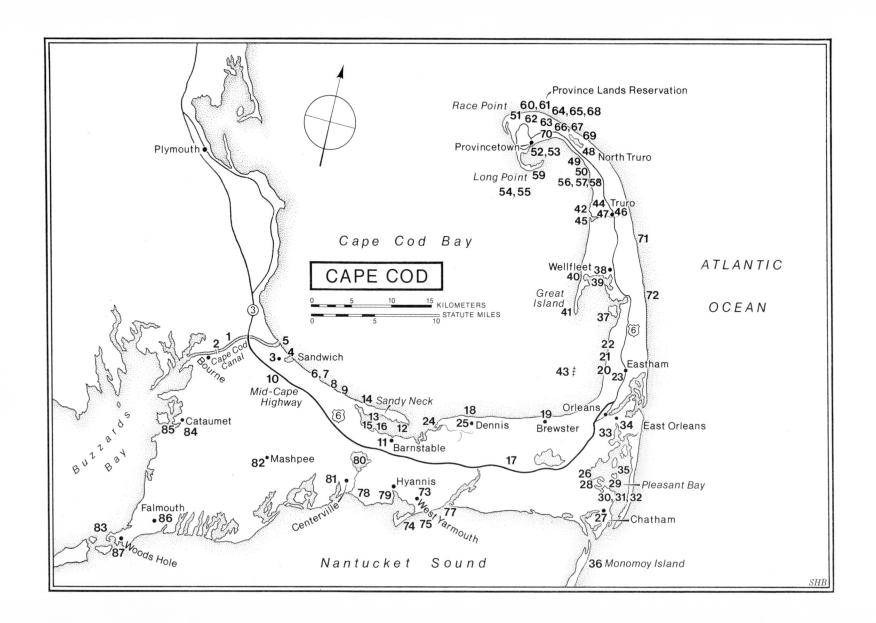

Province Lands Reservation

Race Point

Plymouth

Cape Cod Bay

CAPE COD

60,61 64,65,68
51 62 63 66,67
70 69
52,53 48 North Truro
49
50
56,57,58
54,55 59
Long Point

44 Truro
42 47 46
45

71

ATLANTIC

OCEAN

Wellfleet 38
40 39

Great Island
41 37

72

0   5   10   15 KILOMETERS
0   5   10 STATUTE MILES

22
21
43 ‡ 20 23 Eastham

1
2 Cape Cod Canal
Bourne

5
3 4 Sandwich

6,7
8 9

10
Mid-Cape Highway

14 *Sandy Neck*

13
15 16 12 24 25 Dennis 18

19 Orleans
Brewster

33 34 East Orleans

Cataumet
85 84

11 Barnstable

17

82 Mashpee

80

26 35
28 29 *Pleasant Bay*

30,31,32

81 Hyannis

78 79 73
West Yarmouth
74 75 77

27 Chatham

Falmouth
86

83

87 Woods Hole

Nantucket Sound

36 *Monomoy Island*

SHB

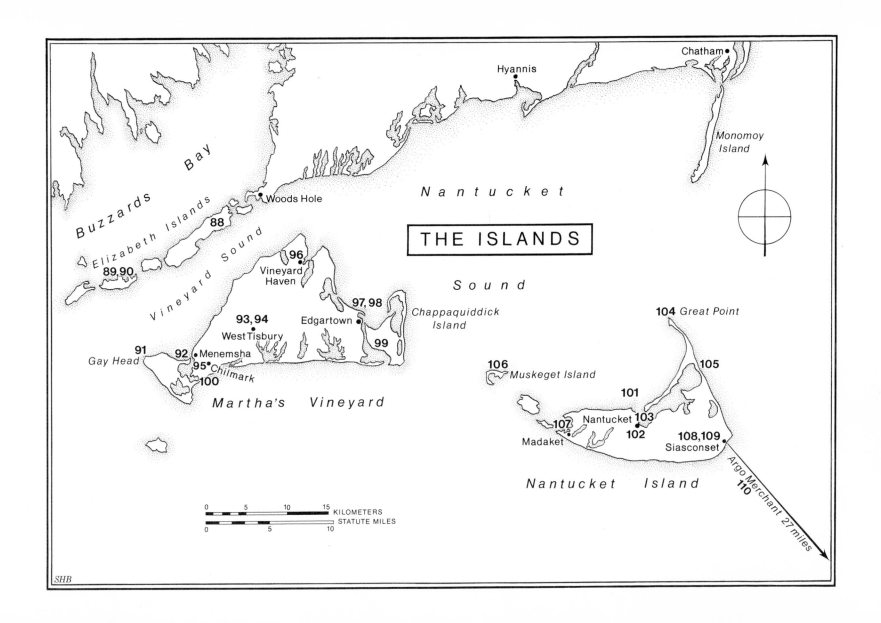

THE ISLANDS

Buzzards Bay

Nantucket

Sound

Chatham

Hyannis

Monomoy Island

Woods Hole

Elizabeth Islands

88

Vineyard Sound

89,90

96

Vineyard Haven

97,98

Chappaquiddick Island

93,94

West Tisbury

Edgartown

99

91

Gay Head

92 Menemsha

95 Chilmark

100

Martha's Vineyard

104 *Great Point*

105

106 *Muskeget Island*

101

107

103

Nantucket

102

108,109
Siasconset

Madaket

Nantucket Island

Argo Merchant 27 miles

110

0   5   10   15   KILOMETERS

STATUTE MILES

0   5   10

SHB

INTRODUCTION

NORTON H. NICKERSON

"Cape Cod!" The very words convey an almost indescribable, privately proud feeling of wonder, mystery, beauty, and thanksgiving to those of us privileged to grow up there. The cheery sound of the first spring peepers on a calm April night, the sight of herring (alewives) fighting their way up rushing brooks in May to the quiet ponds to spawn, the elvers (young eels) passing through these same almost still brooks in August, and the formations of honking geese and swift-winged ducks on their journey south in October — all of these and many more images besides are recalled in the sounds of those two simple words.

Now we have Stephen Proehl's book providing a new perspective to our views and memories of the Cape, a view that heretofore only a few of us have been privileged to see, let alone study in a leisurely fashion. The world of the soaring gull, the busy tern, the quietly circling hawk, and the sometimes noisy crow has been temporarily invaded, but not destroyed; captured but not disturbed. Recorded on film in a range of phenomenally beautiful lights, shadows, and colors of both natural scenes and manmade objects, these aerial photographs give the Cape a new and exciting aspect.

Often spoken of as a bulwark against the mighty North Atlantic (as indeed it is, but not without cost to its sea cliffs and beaches), the Cape, as seen through Mr. Proehl's camera lens, shows us some of the endless variety and patterns of change in marshes, sand flats, and dunes, recalling at every tide and on every blustery day the magnificence of Tennyson's words written about presumably more solid geography:

> *The hills are shadows, and they flow*
> *From form to form and nothing stands;*
> *They melt like mists, the solid lands,*
> *Like clouds they shape themselves and go.*

Although the actual snapping of a shutter is a purely mechanical action, the beauty of the finished product must of necessity reflect the sense of design and both the recognition and genuine appreciation of its subject that the experienced mind can bring to bear. Mr. Proehl's mastery of aerial photography as well as his understanding of the significance of the Cape to his viewers are skillfully blended in page after page of contemporary scenes which at once signify history and foretell the future.

Consider how magnificent a journey unfolds in these pictures: a trip down the north- and east-facing shores the full length of the Cape, and then along the bayshore beach, over to Monomoy Wildlife Preserve, along the south shore of the Cape, and over to the Elizabeth Islands, Martha's Vineyard, and then Nantucket, to end in the enigma of a recently grounded oil tanker. Is it any wonder that we find the sea-land relationship fascinating, unpredictable, and alive with beauty? Is it any wonder that we find ourselves envying the creatures of the air for which this deeply three-dimensional quality is a continuing perspective?

The pictures of the Cape Cod Canal, its bridges, and its jetties demonstrate the engineering marvels of mankind. The highway bridges themselves offer to the road traveler tantalizing vistas of the very things this whole photographic collection is about.

Other photos portray the striking natural beauty of salt marshes laced with creeks and shimmering salt ponds. Their appearance from above gives no sign of their importance in several other ways.

They serve as food sources for our teeming offshore fisheries, many species of which also use these biologically rich areas as nurseries for their young. The great deposits of peat which have been formed beneath these marshes serve to separate and slow the loss of fresh ground water from the coastal lands to the salty waters of the ocean. These peats also serve as natural filters, removing poisonous nitrates and organism pollutants such as DDT, so they can no longer circulate endlessly through the food chains of which we too are part. Storm wave energy is dissipated by the thousands of stiff grass blades of a healthy marsh, and no manmade breakwater has yet been devised which repairs itself by continued growth as do the marshes. Some of these creeks lead upward to inland fresh ponds, forming the waterways up which the alewives ascend to their freshwater spawning grounds. Their fry spend six to eight weeks as miniature vacuum cleaners, voraciously eating all the microscopic water plants they can find, and then drift down to the ocean, returning three years later as adults to repeat the cycle in the very pond in which they began. Mr. Proehl's pictures, of course, being but one glimpse in a time continuum, cannot show such hidden details, but they clearly indicate how intimately the coastal ecosystems are entwined with one another.

Still other shots, such as that of the *Argo Merchant* wreck, speak to both the awesome power of the sea and the tragedy of abuse by human-created oil spills. Sadly, we have no technology sufficient to recover even a fraction of the oil spilled in the harsh winter seas of this area, yet we are pressing forward ominously with offshore explorations on the Georges Bank, one of the most bountiful fishing areas in the world, with more spills inevitable. Just because we have not looked for and hence not found any biological effect of the *Argo Merchant*'s spilled oil, does it mean, as the editor of the prestigious journal *Science* concluded, that there is none, that we are free to pollute the vast ocean as we please? Or are we seeing in this book perhaps the last pictures of fishing boats in clear waters, green productive marshes, sparkling bays, gleaming dunes, and clean oil-free beaches? At the time of the *Argo Merchant*'s grounding, the ocean, mercifully, was running eastward in the very area where constant monitoring since then has shown westward currents without interruption for the past six years. Perhaps the *Argo Merchant* spill is an implicit warning that even the beautiful endless variety of changing land-water relationships shown here can be undone by a mankind that cares only for the concern of the moment.

I predict that these photographs will go beyond their strong immediate impression of breathtaking epic artistry, that they will raise the consciousness of their viewers to a level where caring about the continued presence of this fragile shoreline beauty will make each reader want to participate in some of the continuing efforts at both private and governmental levels to keep unsullied these lands which gave the Pilgrims their first impressions of the New World.

South Dennis, Massachusetts
May 1978

PART I

OUT THE NORTH SIDE

From the Bourne Bridge to Provincetown

Plate 1

4

5

8 9

10

11

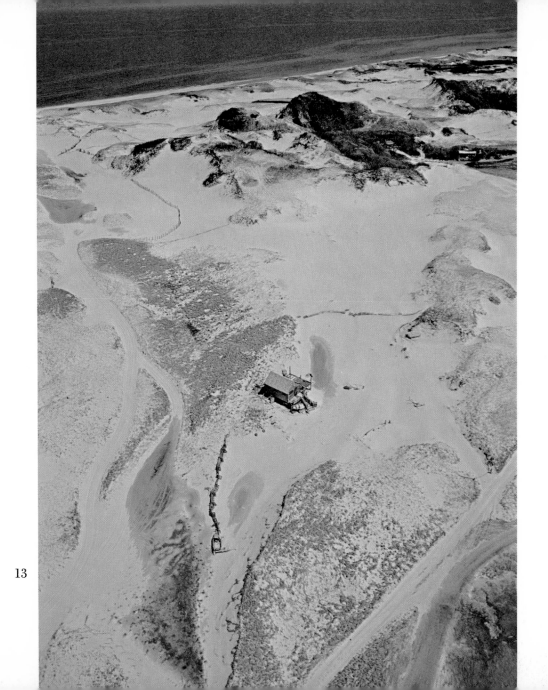

12

13

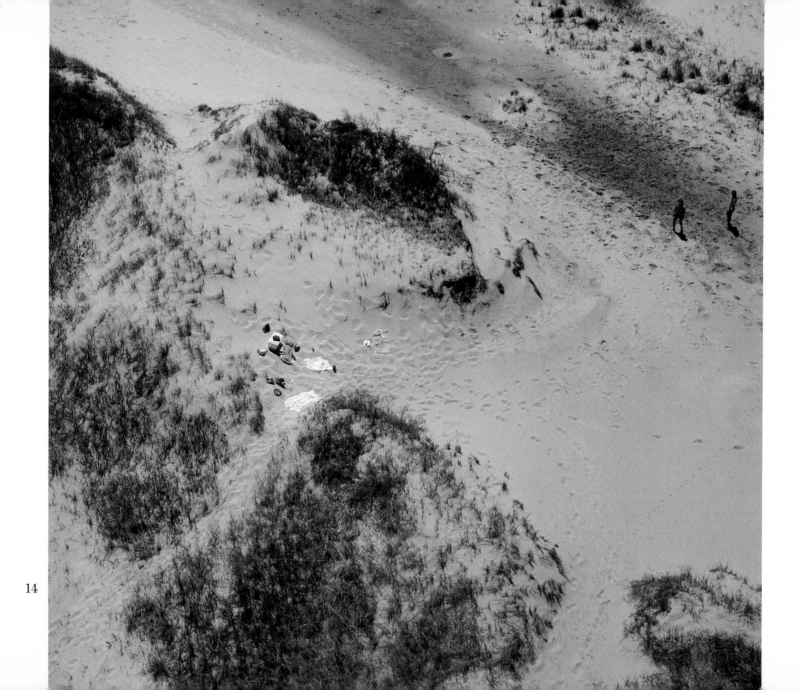

14

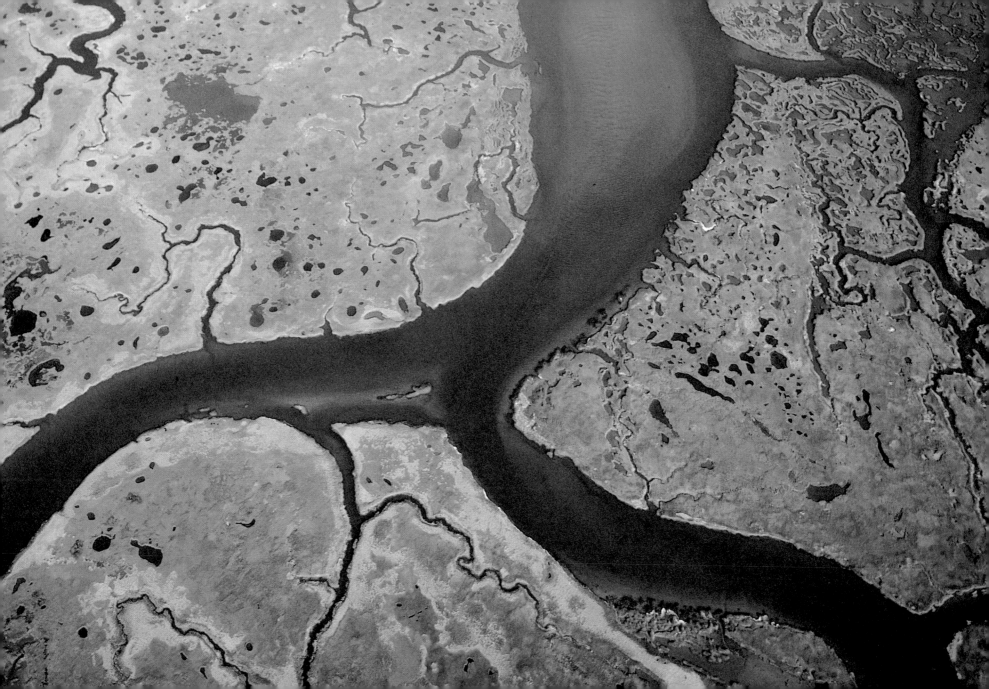

17

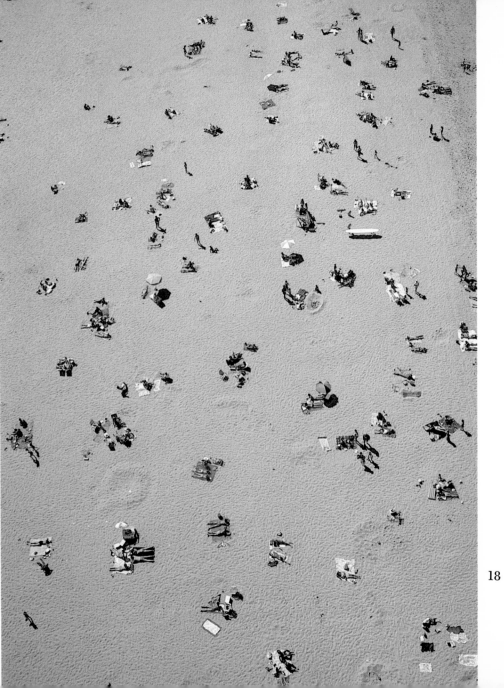

18

19

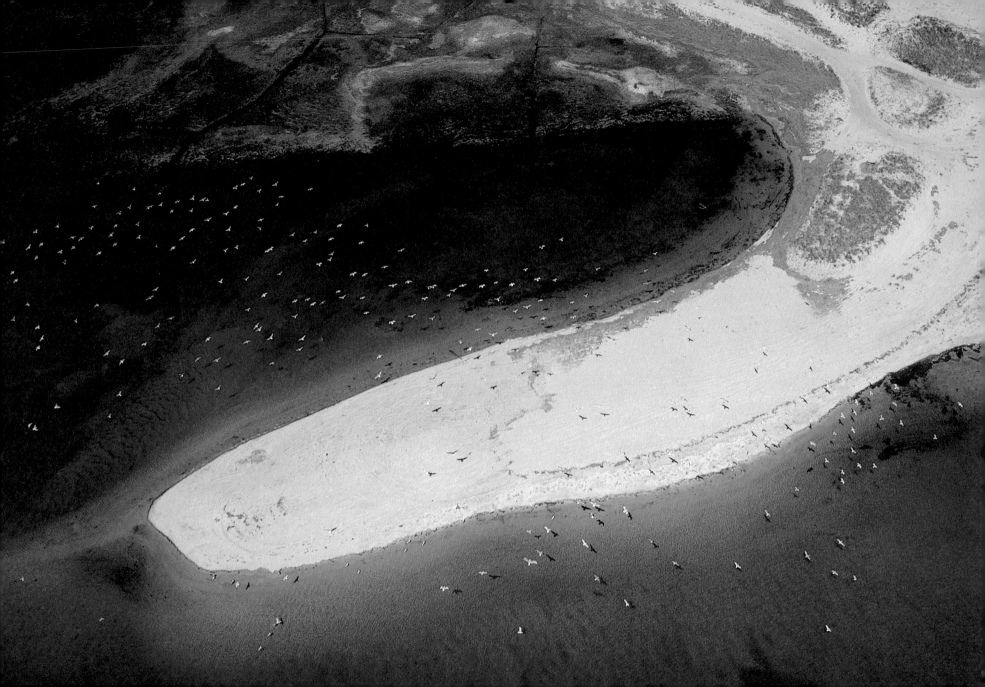

22

23

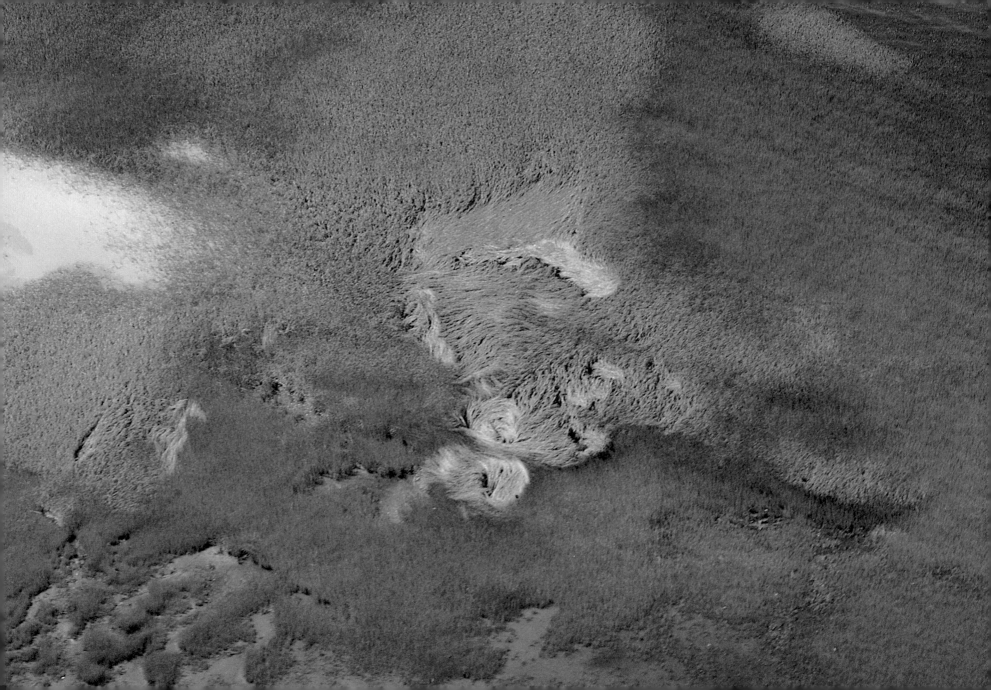

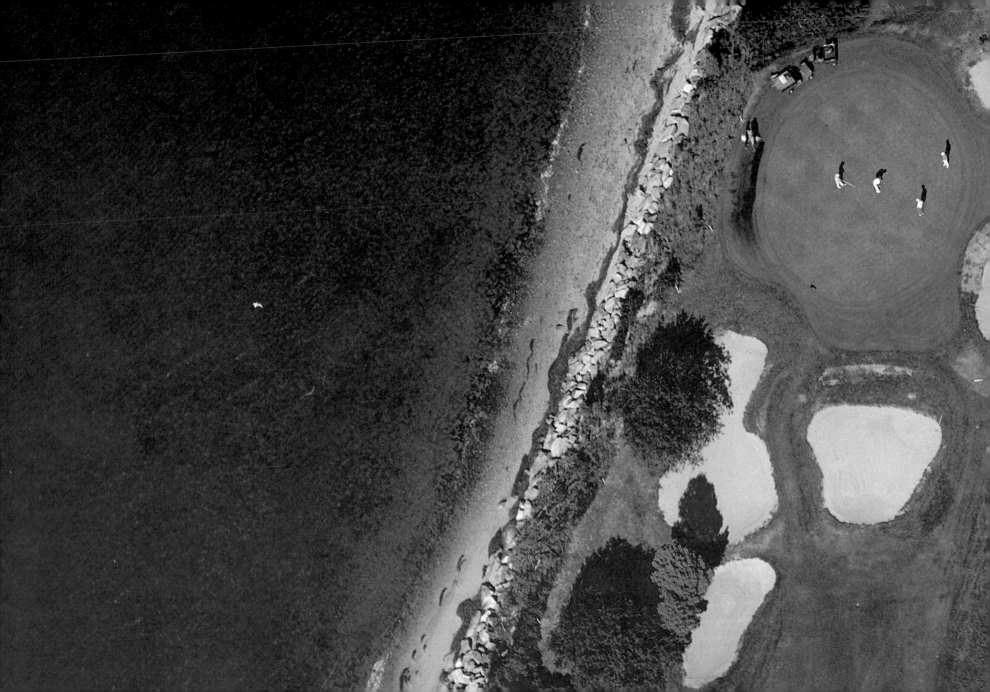

27 28

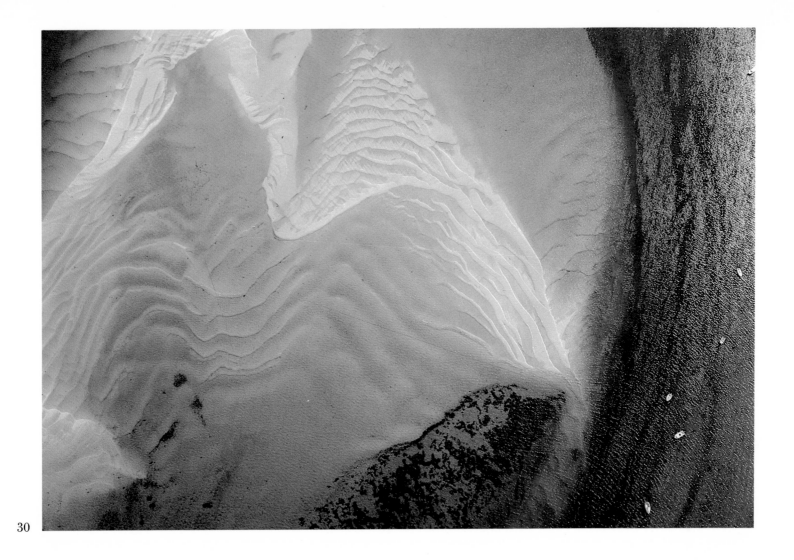

29 30

32

33

35

36

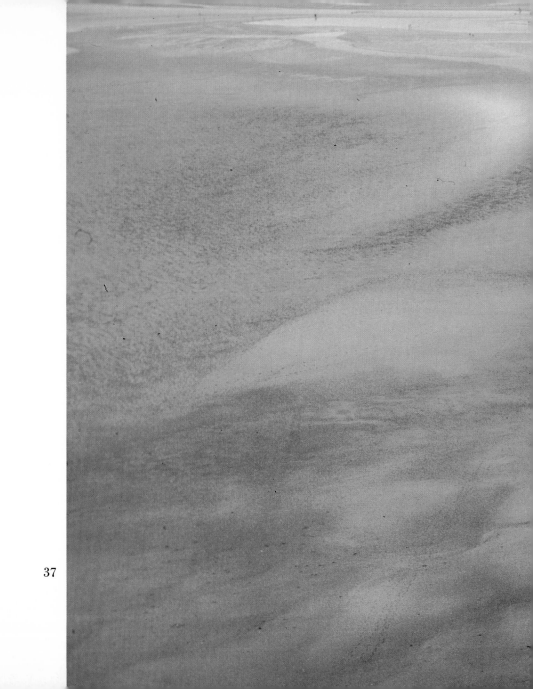

37

40

41

43

44

49

53

60

61

64

65

70

71   72

BACK ON THE SOUTH SIDE

From Provincetown to Woods Hole

73

74

75

76

77

80

84

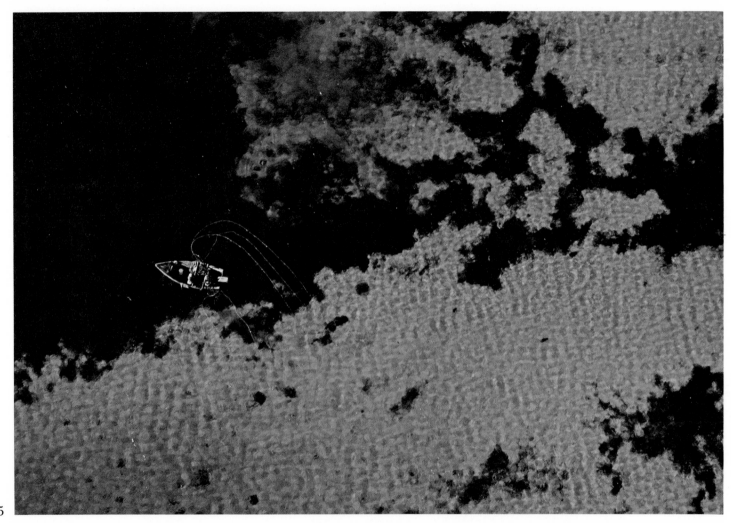

85

THE ISLANDS

The Elizabeth Islands, Martha's Vineyard, and Nantucket

89

94

95

96

102

110

NOTES ON THE PLATES
BIBLIOGRAPHY
TECHNICAL NOTES

NOTES TO THE PLATES

PART I

1. Looking west over the Cape Cod Canal toward Bourne. The Bourne Bridge can be seen in the foreground and, behind that, the old rail-road bridge. I took this photograph from about 600 feet in late fall. With the coming of winter, the water begins to take on the subtle, colorless hues of the land around it.

2. Along with the Sagamore, the Bourne Bridge carries you over from the mainland and marks the gateway to the Cape and the Islands.

3. The town of Sandwich, with Shawme Pond in the foreground. As I was heading home toward Boston after a day of disappointing weather, the sun slid through and made a short appearance for the departed residents of Sandwich.

4. This abstract study depicts the light and dark of shoaling. In shallow water, the sand reflects more light; where it is deeper it becomes darker. The same picture taken a year later would show that the shoal lines had shifted.

5. On the bayside entrance to the Cape Cod Canal, this distinct geometric pattern is immediately apparent to the aerial observer. The tide normally flows from this entrance to the south with as much as a six-foot difference in water level between the two ends. The manmade breakwater keeps the canal free from drifting sand that would otherwise close it.

6. Photography in its simplest terms is nothing more than the absence and presence of light, and in this photograph of Old Harbor Creek in Sandwich that theory seems to support itself. As in Plate 3, the sun has once again touched down, this time highlighting a row of summer cottages. I sometimes asked Dean, the helicopter pilot, to circle slowly over a subject while we waited for the sun to break through. More often though, this kind of photograph offers itself by chance.

7. Looking out from Sandwich Harbor.

8. A cloud momentarily passes over the shoreline in Sandwich as Sandy Neck and the Great Marshes stretch out in the background.

9. A side road branches to the bay in Barnstable. The single road is like a line of children hiking to the sea: when they glimpse the water they dash for it, each on his own path.

10. Up and down the spine, the Mid-Cape Highway carries most travelers, who at some point leave it for the seclusion of their own hideaway. By design or necessity, the construction of the major artery down the middle of the Cape has protected the remoteness of the shores.

11. A trio of late autumn golfers on a course in Barnstable. At 500 feet, I often wonder how close to the hole I could place a golfball from the helicopter.

131

12. An old summer colony at the tip of Sandy Neck. In all my flying over the Cape and the Islands, I found this to be the most authentic example of an old seaside village. Untouched by the modern world, it reveals no traces of the automobile.

13. Boarded up for the winter on Sandy Neck. This solitary cottage faces a losing battle against the ravages of windblown sand.

14. A familiar Cape scene on Sandy Neck. The towels and footprints belonged to four boys who were playing with a Frisbee nearby. As we circled for the shot, one of them hurled the blue disk at the helicopter; the wash from the blades forced it down.

15. Calves Pasture Point with Barnstable Harbor on the left. The kettles, or hollows, at the bottom of the picture were formed by glacial action with the melting of the last larger chunks of ice about 50,000 to 70,000 years ago. A geological history of the Cape and the Islands makes fascinating reading. A good reference is Arthur N. Strahler's *A Geologist's View of Cape Cod*.

16. Without reference to some kind of human scale it is difficult to orient oneself in this photograph. It could have been taken at 50,000 feet or under a microscope. Actually, it was taken from an altitude of 800 feet over the Great Marsh. The small kettles average less than ten feet in diameter and provide a place that attracts fish. Any ditching attempts by man would result in a departure of the fish and an increase in the mosquito population.

17. Looking northeast from Brewster, with Long Pond on the right. The ponds to the left of the diagonal land mass drain into the bay, while those on the right drain out of the Herring River to the south. A windless day causes clouds to form in mirror-like fashion above the land.

18. A beach in Brewster.

19. A row of summer houses in Brewster with a view to the bay. Dr. Nickerson commented that a slight zigzag in the straight paths leading from the cottages would avert the scouring of sand that is taking place with the movement of the tides.

20. A spit of sand covered with seagulls protrudes into the Herring River in Eastham.

21. This photograph, taken on a creek inlet in Eastham, shows extensive shoaling produced by underwater currents. The turquoise-green color and the clarity of the water are suggestive of a Caribbean seascape.

22–23. A higher perspective reveals the lacework of grasses, tidal creeks, kettles, and shoals that make up this inner salt marsh in Eastham. I took over 100 frames of this spot, finding different patterns and compositions with each pass.

24. A footbridge crosses Quivett Creek in Dennis.

25. A close-up of cowlick grasses in Dennis. This common Cape grass is thin-stemmed and falls over from its own weight when it reaches a couple of feet in height. The name of the grass derives from its appearance: it looks as though it has been licked by a cow.

26. This hole at Eastward Ho Golf Course on Nickerson's Neck presents a formidable challenge to this group. It's encircled by five sandtraps and Pleasant Bay.

27. A small boatworks in Chatham, with Nauset Beach in the background.

28. A long shot of the Eastward Ho, including the main clubhouse and paddle-tennis courts. Crow's Pond lies on the other side.

29. Over Pleasant Bay in Chatham we see an underwater sand dune.

30. A good example of the preliminary stages of marsh formation. Some of the shoals have built up and broken the surface of the water to form a base from which grasses can grow. The uneven formation of the shoal lines has been caused by erratic water currents which, in turn, have been influenced by the wind and tides.

31. Taken with a 21mm wide-angle lens, this photograph shows Pleasant Bay in various stages of salt-marsh development. Where sufficient

sand has accumulated, islands with vegetation have been established. Eventually the whole bay will become a salt marsh.

32. A view to the north, with Tern Island on the left and Nauset Beach in the upper right.

33. A controlled burn takes place on Fort Hill in Eastham to keep down brush. In the past, this area was grazed by cattle.

34. A close-up of Salt Pond Bay.

35. Three of the dynamic environments that created and sustain the Cape are shown here: the ocean, the barrier beach, and the marsh. The beach at Nauset has been formed by the continual southward deposit of sand from the ocean currents. With the buildup of the barrier beach a protracted region has been formed where the start of a marsh is taking place.

36. Monomoy Island, extending into Nantucket Sound south of Chatham. The end of Nauset Beach, in the upper right, is building toward Monomoy at about 20 feet a year. The salt pond in the left foreground has recently been sealed from the ocean. It will, over the next few years, gradually change from salt to fresh, as the rains accumulate. The smaller pond on the right is fresh.

37. There is something intriguing about walking over land that seemingly belongs under water. In a sense, it is like walking on water. These people are enjoying such a walk on flats in Wellfleet. We landed the helicopter, unable to resist the temptation ourselves.

38. The town of Wellfleet, with the Atlantic Ocean in the east.

39. A couple has a secluded section of Great Island in Wellfleet Harbor all to themselves. This island is part of the Cape Cod National Seashore.

40. Against the backdrop of a painter's brushstroke, a small sailboat skims the waters off Wellfleet.

41. The eroding sands at Jeremy Point attest to the fate of Billingsgate Island, an island that a hundred years ago lay three quarters of a mile off Jeremy Point. The island consisted of over thirty homes, a school, and a lighthouse. As the tides steadily rose, the residents evacuated the island with their possessions, including their houses, which they floated to the mainland.

42. This gentleman appears to have staked out his own island near the Harbor Bar in Truro. His claim will disappear with the next high tide.

43. This old Liberty Ship that ran aground off Wellfleet was up to a short while ago used for bombing practice. Its present mission is the support of a lobster population. Lobster buoys surround the vessel.

44. Two boys portage a Sailfish over a flat into the mouth of the Pamet River in Truro. Their barefoot, Huck Finn adventure symbolizes my impressions of the Cape and the Islands.

45. The entrance to the Pamet River in Truro, with the Town Landing in the background. What is left of the old railroad to Provincetown can be seen as a white streak that doglegs to the upper right.

46. Thousands of years ago the Pamet Valley extended out to sea for another two miles. Over the years, the tidal currents eroded the valley to its present size, leaving the river with little land to drain. Now the level and salinity of the river are influenced by the tides which come from the entrance (Plate 45) and the rains which accumulate in the area seen here.

47. At low tide in the Pamet River. The lower end of the valley is drained and tobacco-colored waters filter out of the marsh.

48. Pilgrim Lake was once open to the bay and known as East Harbor until it was diked in the late 1800s to maintain a land connection between North Truro and Provincetown. At that time, the only overland route to Provincetown was a swiftly eroding beach on the ocean side.

49. Looking north along Pilgrim Beach toward Provincetown. Jetties built from the shore have filled with sand.

50. Provincetown and Long Point from an altitude of 5000 feet. The Cape is like a huge whale with its back out of water. Our concept of land versus water on the Cape is as flimsy as a small boat at sea, or the rise and fall of a whale. What so short a time ago was water is now land, and what was land has now become water.

51. The lower arm of the Cape. Provincetown Airport, seen in the foreground, provides easy access for the throngs of visitors who spend the summer months here.

52–53. Provincetown Beach at high tide.

54. About five miles off Long Point. This leisure craft is almost hidden by the texture of the water.

55. Also off Long Point in the same fishing ground as in Plate 61, lines trail the *Andy-Lynn* in search of tuna. Her occupants appear to have little concern over the matter.

56–57. Sunbathing and building sand castles on the shoals near Provincetown.

58. The bay is so shallow and clear these sailboats reflect their shadows on the floor of the bay. The photograph was taken near Provincetown Harbor.

59. The boats racing around Long Point appear to be in their last lap as they head for the finish and come into Provincetown Harbor. A boater's paradise, the Cape and the Islands play host to sailors from around the world.

60. The parking lot at Race Point Coast Guard Station. A colorful array of cars spills like a river into the sea.

61. A paved bicycle trail in the Province Lands area meanders for eight miles through dunes, forests, and ponds. Several beaches are on its path, including Herring Cove and Race Point.

62. A look across the dunes to the west. Forests such as these were logged extensively by early settlers, causing the sand to blow into Provincetown. When the townspeople realized their folly they planted grasses and small trees to keep from being buried.

63. Horseback riding in the Province Lands. When we flew closer to the riders, the leader broke off and executed a perfectly symmetrical figure eight. The eye of the camera brings out the best in everybody.

64. A four-wheel vehicle makes its way back to the beachside settlement at Race Point. Vehicles are required to stay on designated trails to avoid damage to the dunes.

65. These modern-day adventurers, reversing the westward direction of their ancestors, have reached the last frontier at Race Point. The Cape Cod National Seashore limits the number of campers to 125 at any given time by issuing three-day permits.

66. A summer cottage at Race Point Beach.

67. The inhabitants of the orange tent were probably relaxing at nearby Race Point Beach.

68. The eastward approach to the tip of Cape Cod. The colonists first landed on these shores before pressing on to historic Plymouth Rock.

69. Two ladies and their shadows stride on the beach at High Head.

70. High on a dune in the Province Lands, this young man waves as if to plead for water. He was, in fact, enjoying the solitude he had discovered.

71. Newcomb Hollow Beach in Wellfleet. Undercutting by storm waves has left steep slopes of loose dry sand. Running and playing on the slopes can cause the sand to slide toward the sea, where it is swiftly carried away by tidal currents. In this particular vicinity of the Cape the tidal currents hit shore from opposite directions. Shoredrifting of sand that flows to the north is building up the Race Point and Long Point areas, and sand moving to the south is extending Monomoy Point.

72. Sand script at Marconi Beach in South Wellfleet.

PART II

73. This view to the east includes West Yarmouth and, beyond that, Barnstable. In the upper right is Hyannis Airport, a favorite watering

hole for the pilot and me. We give the airport diner and the refueling service a four-star rating.

74. Great Island and Lewis Bay in West Yarmouth. Barely visible in the far distance are the Elizabeth Islands.

75. A boat hangs on a precipice of shoals near Great Island.

76. An interesting study of wave refraction in Nantucket Sound. Trails left by boats can be seen long after their departure.

77. The Bass River, like the Pamet, flows two ways: in on the flow tide and out on the ebb tide. The Bass River Golf Club commands a spectacular site on the banks.

78. A golf green sitting at the edge of a marsh in Barnstable creates a striking contrast between natural and manmade land forms.

79. The Kennedy compound in Hyannis photographed in late afternoon.

80. Wequaquet Lake, a freshwater pond, crowds around the edges of a sumptuous retreat in Barnstable. Not subject to coastal erosion, the grounds are in little danger.

81. Facing onto Centerville Harbor, these estates along Craigville Beach are representative of the way of life on this stretch of the Cape.

82. A planned development of summer and year-round cottages form a maze-like pattern in Mashpee. Mashpee has been the focus of a highly controversial lawsuit involving the claims of native Indians to ownership of thousands of acres in the town.

83. The Falmouth Airport, carved out of the woods like a remote jungle airstrip, is photographed in late fall. The oak trees, which are a bright orange, will in time replace the pines. The hardwoods can survive in the shade of the pines; the pines, however, cannot survive in the shade of the hardwoods.

84. An estate in Cataumet looking in the direction of Wing's Neck.

85. Fishermen tend to their lines on the waters of Megansett Harbor in Falmouth.

86. A panoramic view of Woods Hole with Buzzard's Bay on the left and Vineyard Sound on the right.

87. A close-up of the Woods Hole Oceanographic Institute. The ship on the left is visiting from a campus in California. This area is a beehive of activity during the summer with a mix of students, scientists, and tourists. Woods Hole is also the home of the Marine Biological Laboratory and the National Fisheries Service.

PART III

88. The Elizabeth Islands, backlit by an afternoon sun, extend in a southwesterly direction out from Woods Hole. The entire chain of islands is virtually uninhabited and is owned by a single family.

89–90. Two photographs of muted autumn color on one of the Elizabeth Islands.

91. The Gay Head Cliffs on Martha's Vineyard. The Cape and the Islands date back 10,000 years except for this section, which contains deposits of cretaceous clays over 100 million years old. Precipitation and tidal currents are eroding a vein of red clay which trails out to sea.

92. The village of Menemsha on Gay Head.

93–94. Very similar in appearance to an inland Massachusetts farming community is the town of West Tisbury. Glacial disturbance was minimal on the Islands, leaving a rich soil for the support of agricultural activities, including grape growing.

95. A cluster of modern homes in Chilmark.

96. A view of Vineyard Haven and the harbor. Across Vineyard Sound the shores of Cape Cod lie barely visible.

97. The ferry carries a single automobile from Edgartown to Chappaquiddick Island. The ferry is called *On Time* because it makes the three-minute trip when and if it wants to.

98. These stately capes overlook Edgartown Harbor.

99. The south shore of Martha's Vineyard. A barrier beach made up of heavy clay protects these fresh ponds that are rich in oysters. There are occasional openings to the ocean that maintain the salinity at the right level for survival of the oysters. Too much fresh water and the oysters will die; too much salt and parasites are introduced.

100. Sunset over Gay Head and the tip of the Elizabeth Islands.

101. The Nantucket ferry slices into the sound at the start of its two-hour trip to Hyannis.

102. The town of Nantucket. In the early 1800s this village of quaint colonial houses, cobblestoned streets, museums, and art galleries was the whaling center of the industry. "Nantucket" comes from an Indian word meaning "the faraway land."

103. Another ferry makes its way out of Nantucket Harbor; this one is headed for Woods Hole. Coatue Point sweeps in from the right.

104. Recently closed off from the sea, this pond on Great Point is undergoing a conversion from salt to fresh water. The accumulation of rainwater forces the saltwater out through the sides of the pond. As sand deposits increase the width of the sides of the pond, saltwater intrusion decreases. The combination of the rain and sand deposits will eventually produce a totally fresh pond.

105. A view to the southwest shows the length of Nantucket Harbor protected by Coatue Beach. The cusps pointing into the Harbor have been cut by winds blowing from the southwest in the summer and the northeast in the winter.

106. Muskeget Island, off the western end of Nantucket Island, has a slight resemblance to the shape of the United States and the Caribbean Islands.

107. Not more than a decade ago, a hurricane cut off this small spit of land from Madaket. It appears like a large fish about to eat a smaller one.

108. The beautifully laid-out town of Siasconset sits at the easternmost edge of Nantucket — next stop, the coast of Spain.

109. The clay courts of a tennis club in Siasconset are actively occupied in mid-September.

110. The *Argo Merchant* comes to rest on the shoals 27 miles southeast of Nantucket. This photograph was taken December 22, 1976, the morning after the oil tanker split in two and disgorged the bulk of her cargo.

BIBLIOGRAPHY

Beston, Henry. *The Outermost House.* New York: The Viking Press, Inc., 1962.

Chamberlain, Barbara. *These Fragile Outposts: A Geological Look at Cape Cod, Martha's Vineyard, and Nantucket.* New York: Doubleday & Company, Inc., 1964.

Hay, John. *The Great Beach.* New York: Ballantine Books, Inc., 1972.
———. *The Sandy Shore.* Old Greenwich, Connecticut: The Chatham Press, Inc., 1968.

Kittredge, Henry C. *Cape Cod: Its People and Their History.* Boston: Houghton Mifflin Company, 1968.

Leonard, Jonathan N. *Atlantic Beaches.* New York: Time-Life Books, 1972.

Richardson, Wyman. *The House on Nauset Marsh.* Old Greenwich, Connecticut: The Chatham Press, Inc., 1972.

Sadlier, Paul, and Ruth Sadlier. *Short Walks on Cape Cod and the Vineyard.* Chester, Connecticut: Pequot Press, Inc., 1976.

Strahler, Arthur N. *A Geologist's View of Cape Cod.* Garden City, N.Y.: Natural History Press, Doubleday & Company, Inc., 1966.

Teal, John, and Mildred Teal. *Life and Death of a Salt Marsh.* New York: Ballantine Books, Inc., 1974.

Thoreau, Henry D. *Cape Cod.* Edited by Dudley C. Lunt. New Haven: College and University Press, 1951.

TECHNICAL NOTES

Taking photographs from a helicopter presupposes a particular set of technical conditions regarding the platform (in this case, the helicopter) and photographic equipment. The pictures in this book were taken from a three-seater Enstrom helicopter, which affords a wide-angle view between the aircraft's landing skids and the main rotor blades. The wide-angle view is important because the constant flexing of rotor blades in and out of the shot minimizes the picture area. Much of the success or failure of a series of shots depends on the ability of the pilot to quickly give the photographer a window when an appealing subject comes into view. This involves pointing the photographer and camera, placed at right angles to the vector of the helicopter, toward the shot — which usually translates into a crabbing action that demands considerable skill from the pilot. Removing the door from the passenger side of the 'copter allows the photographer to avoid reflections and distortions. An ideal minimum shutter speed of 1/250 overcomes any vibration from the aircraft. In turn, the high shutter speeds require medium-to-fast-speed films; Kodachrome 64 and Ektachrome 200 with the ASA overrated for slight underexposure produce good results.

The camera equipment for this book includes two motorized Nikons and four lenses: a 21mm, 28mm, 35mm, and an 85mm. Keeping equipment and procedures as simple and standardized as possible is a good rule for all photography and is especially important in the hectic airborne environment of a helicopter.

S.P.

139